SQUADRON

No. 10

The North American
Mustang Mk. IV
in Western Europe

Phil H. LISTEMANN

ISBN: 978-2918590-70-5

Copyright

© 2015 Philedition - Phil Listemann

www.RAF-IN-COMBAT.com

Colour profiles: Gaetan Marie/Bravo Bravo Aviation

All right reserved. No part of this book may be reproduced, stored in a retrieval system or transmitted in any form by any means, electronic, mechanical, photocopying, recording or otherwise, without prior permission of the author.

Contributors & Acknowledgments:
André Bar, Steve Brooking, Bill Coffman, Andrew Thomas, **Wilhelm Ratuszynski**

GLOSSARY OF TERMS

PERSONEL :
(AUS)/RAF: Australian serving in the RAF
(BEL)/RAF: Belgian serving in the RAF
(CAN)/RAF: Canadian serving in the RAF
(CZ)/RAF: Czechoslovak serving in the RAF
(NFL)/RAF: Newfoundlander serving in the RAF
(NL)/RAF: Dutch serving in the RAF
(NZ)/RAF: New Zealander serving in the RAF
(POL)/RAF: Pole serving in the RAF
(RHO)/RAF: Rhodesian serving in the RAF
(SA)/RAF: South African serving in the RAF
(US)/RAF - RCAF : American serving in the RAF or RCAF

RANKS
G/C : Group Captain
W/C : Wing Commander
S/L : Squadron Leader
F/L : Flight Lieutenant
F/O : Flying Officer
P/O : Pilot Officer
W/O : Warrant Officer
F/Sgt : Flight Sergeant
Sgt : Sergeant
Cpl : Corporal
LAC : Leading Aircraftman

OTHER
ATA: Air Transport Auxiliary
CO : Commander
DFC : Distinguished Flying Cross
DFM : Distinguished Flying Medal
DSO : Distinguished Service Order
Eva. : Evaded
ORB : Operational Record Book
OTU : Operational Training Unit
PoW : Prisoner of War
PAF: Polish Air Force
RAF : Royal Air Force
RAAF : Royal Australian Air Force
RCAF : Royal Canadian Air Force
RNZAF : Royal New Zealand Air Force
SAAF : South African Air Force
s/d: Shot down
Sqn : Squadron
† : Killed

CODENAMES - OFFENSIVE OPERATIONS - FIGHTER COMMAND

CIRCUS:
Bombers heavily escorted by fighters, the purpose being to bring enemy fighters into combat.

RAMROD:
Bombers escorted by fighters, the primary aim being to destroy a target.

RANGER:
Large formation freelance intrusion over enemy territory with aim of wearing down enemy figthers.

RHUBARD:
Freelance fighter sortie against targets of opportunity.

RODEO:
A fighter sweep without bombers.

SWEEP:
An offensive flight by fighters designed to draw up and clear the enemy from the sky.

THE MUSTANG MK. IV

The North American Mustang belongs to the category of the legendary fighters of WWII. The Mustang IV was the British version of the USAAF P-51D that was introduced during the spring of 1944. This version had the new cockpit canopy that was highly appreciated by the pilots. This one-piece moulded Perspex sliding hood provided very good visibility in the most important direction – rearwards. Another improvement was the armament that increased from four 0.5-in machine guns in the Mustang Mk.III to six in the Mk.IV. A derivative was also put in production, the P-51K, which differed only in the type of propeller fitted. The latter became the Mustang IVA in the RAF inventory. The RAF had long wanted the Mustang for its units based in England, the Middle East and the Far East but, as priority was given to the USAAF Fighter Groups, it was not until very late in 1944 that these new Mustangs were released to the RAF.

The British received two Mustang P-51Ds (TK586 and TK589) from USAAF stock for evaluation in July 1944. They were from the very first batches, Block Five, and were formerly 44-13524 and 44-13332. The British took delivery between September 1944 and January 1945 of thirty Mustang Mk.IVs, with serials KH641 to KH670 (ex 44-11168 to 11187 and 44-11253 to 11262), and 200 Mustang Mk.IVAs, with serials KH671 to KH870 (ex 44-11374 to 11413 and 44-11478 to 11517). This was the balance of the 450 Mustang III previously ordered but only the first 220 were delivered as Mk.IIIs. These Mk.IVs were diverted from the North American Aviation plant in Dallas, Texas, and all were Block Five models. The Mk.IVAs built at the same plants were diverted from Block One (80) and Block Five (120). One of these, KH660, crashed before delivery at its home base of Dallas on 23 August 1944. It crashed during a test flight and its pilot, First Lieutenant Joseph W. Garard, was killed.

The first Mustang IVs to be introduced into RAF inventory were TK586 and TK589 in June 1944 (for testing). Below: 44-13332, still with its USAAF serial, later changed to TK589. Both were former P-51D-5s built at Inglewood in California and would the only RAF Mustangs built at the original North American plant. The rest of the RAF's Mustang IV and IVA supply would be built at the North American plant at Dallas, Texas. Up to the P-51D-20, the Mustang was mainly used as a fighter while from the P-51D-25 its fighter-bomber capabilities were improved with the introduction of underwing hardpoints for five-inch rockets or two 500 or 1,000-lb bombs.
(Phil Butler)

Another view of 44-13332 (TK589) at Boscombe Down. *(Phil Butler)*

Later on the British could order, via Lend-Lease, another batch of 900 Mustang Mk.IV/Mk.IVAs was ordered and delivered in the sequence after the last Mustang from the previous batch. The serials allocated were KM100 to KM492 for 392 Mustang Mk.IVAs (172 Block Ten and 181 Block Fifteen, 44-11953 to 11858, 44-12263 to 12433, 44-12552 to 12602, 44-12628 to 12707 and 44-12759 to 12809) and KM493 to KM743 for the 251 Mustang Mk IVs (all Block Twenty, 44-12903 to 12942, 44-12960 to 12999, 44-13050 to 13100, 44-13141 to 13180, 44-13221 to 13252, 44-84391 to 84397, 44-84468, 44-84681 to 84720) delivered until August 1945 when Lend-Lease was terminated. Consequently, the last 56 Mustang IVs (KM744 to KM799) were not delivered and were never shipped to the UK and the balance KM744 to KM999 never built. A further five crashed before delivery. KH689 was later repaired and repossessed by the US. KH839 was lost on a ferry flight within the USA on 10 December 1944 and the same thing happened with KM419 (7 March 1945), KM425 (2 March 1945, its pilot, Flight Officer William A. Quinn was killed) and KM486 (22 March 1945). In all, 869 Mustang Mk.IVs/IVAs were taken on charge by the RAF.

Of those that reached their destination, the UK-based squadrons were the first to take the new Mustang on strength. About 550 were sent to the UK, followed by about 100 for the Mediterranean and then 225 were shipped to the Far East. In the Mediterranean area, including after the war, six RAF squadrons (93, 112, 213, 249, 250 and 260), three SAAF squadrons (1, 2 and 5) and one RAAF squadron (3) used the Mustang Mk.IV as part of the Balkan Air Force. They were flown, in conjunction with the older Mk.IIIs, on fighter-bomber missions. The Mk.III was progressively retired in favour of the newer Mk.IV and the later aircraft remained the only mark used after the war for the squadrons that remained operational until 1947. Within Fighter Command, nine squadrons were fully equipped with the Mk.IV (19, 64, 65, 122, 126, 154, 234, 303 (Polish) and 611) for escort duties before the war ended. No. 154 Squadron was, however, disbanded in March 1945. By VE-Day fifty Mustang Mk.IVs had been struck off charge for various reasons and the Mustang IV continued to serve for a short time. As Lend-Lease terminated in September, all spare parts had to be paid for so the Mustang withdrawal was set, and the squadrons were either disbanded (1 and 2 SAAF in July, 249, 260, 611 and 3 RAAF in August 1945, 5 SAAF in October 1945, 303 in November 1946, 93, 112 and 250 in December 1946), or converted onto British-made aircraft (122 and 234 to Spitfire Mk.IXs in August 1945, 19 and 65 to Spitfire XVIs on March 1946 and May 1946 respectively, 64 to Hornets in May 1946 and 213 to Tempest VIs in February 1947). The Americans, having plenty of Mustangs in various storage facilities, did not ask for the aircraft back and all were scrapped in situ before 1947 ended.

Compared to the US, the usage of the North American P-51D was relatively negligible with about 3500 sorties flown during the war, two-thirds in the Middle East, and few claims made. The main reason for this is that the mark was introduced late in the war, the Americans having supplied their units first, but the Mustang Mk.IV would have played a major role in the RAF had the war against Japan lasted longer. It is worth noting that the RAF was not the only beneficiary of the release of large numbers of P-51D/K in 1945 as the RAAF, RNZAF and NEIAF were all in the process of either converting their units or receiving deliveries of the aircraft. As far as the Fighter Command is concerned, the following serials were allocated for operational usage:

<u>Mk. IV</u>: KH641-659, KH661-670, KM493-524, KM526-537, KM539, KM540, KM542, KM544, KM546, KM547, KM550-552, KM555, KM556, KM558-561, KM563, KM565-568, KM570-572, KM575, KM578-581, KM583, KM588, KM592, KM594, KM596, KM598, KM599, KM602, KM603. *(110)*

<u>Mk. IVA</u>: KH672-676, KH678, KH680, KH682, KH683, KH685-688, KH690, KH691, KH694-698, KH702-704, KH707-709, KH711-715, KH718-722, KH724-730, KH732-735, KH737-739, KH741-744, KH746-748, KH750-754, KH756-775, KH777-790, KH807, KH811, KH812, KH818, KH819, KH822, KH825, KH826, KH829, KH833-836, KH838, KH840, KH841, KH843-845, KH847-850, KH853-855, KH857-860, KH862-870, KM100-103, KM106, KM111-116, KM118, KM120-126, KM128-134, KM137-146, KM148-153, KM155-168, KM170-173, KM175-384, KM386-418, KM420-424, KM426-437, KM439-477, KM479-485, KM487-482. *(509)*

KM219 reached the UK in March 1945. It was built as a P-51K-10-NT (44-12342). The P-51K was a P-51D with an Aeroproducts propeller instead of the usual Hamilton Standard. The Aeroproducts propeller was generally not preferred by most US crew chiefs and many props were not balanced well. Originally ordered on 21 July 1943, 1,500 P-51Ks were produced and one third went to the RAF. The production was split into four blocks. The K-10 was the most produced with 600 being built (172 went to the RAF). It was this block that introduced the underwing hardpoints for five-inch rockets or two bombs. In US service, more than 150 P-51Ks were converted to reconnaissance fighter configuration as F-6Ks while the rest were mainly used in the CBI or Pacific theatres. KM219 was never issued to any operational squadron and was eventually struck off charge on 2 June 1947. Many Mustang IV/IVAs remained unused after their arrival in the UK.

MUSTANG MK IV
PACKARD MERLIN
MARCH 1945

What about the Mustang V? The end of war against the Japanese prevented the usage of the Mustang IV in this theatre and even the last Mustangs IVs on order were cancelled. However, if the war had lasted a bit longer, not only would more Mustang IV/IVAs have been ordered, but the RAF would probably have considered the introduction of the lightweight version of the Mustang to its inventory. At first the RAF received the last of the three XP-51Fs (formerly 43-43334) for evaluation. It received the serial FR409 and the denomination of Mustang V. Arriving in August 1944, it was used for various tests until March 1946 and then stored at No. 38 MU before finally being scrapped in February 1947. One of the two XP-51Gs (43-43336) was also shipped but arrived in June 1945, saw little use and was scrapped in June 1947. In any case, the type was rejected by both the USAAF and the RAF. However, the RAF showed a great interest in the P-51H and one was earmarked (44-64181, the second P-51H-5-NA built) and given the RAF serial KN987. This airframe was delivered to the USAAF on 13 June 1945 and then flown to Newark for subsequent embarkation to the UK which never took place because of the end of the war in Europe. It was still waiting for disposition on 22 January 1946 when it was sent to MacDill AB in Florida. The P-51H was eventually adopted by the USAAF and large quantities were ordered as P-51L-NTs and P-51M-NTs by VE-Day so it can be assumed the RAF would have followed suit if it had received KN987 for evaluation.

Two views of Mustang IV FR409 while being evaluated in the UK.

March 1945
May 1946

Victories - confirmed or probable claims: 11

First operational sortie:
08.03.45
Last operational sortie:
04.05.45

Number of sorties: 229

Total aircraft written-off: 8

Aircraft lost on operations: 5
Aircraft lost in accidents: 3

Squadron code letters:
YT

COMMANDING OFFICERS

S/L Ian G. Stewart (†)	RAF No.43983	RAF	...	25.03.45
S/L John W. Foster	RAF No.134757	RAF	25.03.45	...

SQUADRON USAGE

When No. 65 Squadron received its first Mustang IVs, in March 1945, it had been operating the Mustang III for more than a year and was the first unit to be converted to a Merlin engine version of the Mustang. From January, the squadron had been stationed at Peterhead, north of Aberdeen in Scotland, and the Commanding Officer was S/L Ian Stewart, recently posted in, who had served in North Africa in a tactical reconnaissance unit – No. 225 Squadron – with which he was awarded the DFC. The main task for 65 was to provide escort to Coastal Command attack aircraft (Beaufighters and Mosquitos) which were operating off the coast of Norway regularly.

The new Mk.IV were taken on charge early in March (KH744, KH758 and KH788) and participated in their first mission on the 8th, an escort to thirty Beaufighters for an anti-shipping mission between Utvær and Sandøy, alongside seven Mk.IIIs of the Squadron. It was not a good start, however, as two of the three Mk.IVs had to return early owing to engine trouble (F/L D.M. Davidson in KH744 and F/L G.C.L. Watt in KH758). Otherwise the rest of the mission was uneventful. This mission was to be only one on which the squadron would both types as, during the following days, the more Mk.IVs became operational (KH642, KH644, KH646, KH657, KH678, KH685, KH686, KH695, KH708, KH715, KH724, KH732, KH744, KH754, KH777, KH822 and KH829). No operations were carried out over the next ten days because of weather or cancellation of the mission. The unit returned to operations on 17 March, totally equipped with the Mk.IV, with the CO in his KH732 leading the squadron on an escort of 33 Mosquitos flying an anti-shipping strike to Aalesand. Six ships were attacked and no air opposition was encountered so the squadron returned to base without loss after close to 4.5 hours of flight. On the 20th, 23rd and 24th the squadron was called to provide escort again for either Beaufighters or Mosquitos. All operations proved uneventful with no air opposition being seen. On the 25th, led by the WingCo, W/C Peter R.W. Wickham, the squadron took off at 13:35 to escort 22 Mosquitoes detailed to carry out an anti-shipping strike at Utvær. When crossing out, the formation was attacked by over twenty Fw190s. In the ensuing combat, the CO disappeared, presumably shot down by the German fighters, and was not seen again. It was sad news for the pilots who had already lost their previous CO, S/L Strachan, in a snowstorm when returning from an escort mission on the 29th of January. However, this time, this sad loss was compensated by the destruction of three Fw190s, with one each for F/L F.H. Bradford, F/O

When 'Johnny' Foster (in the middle with the scarf) took charge of the squadron, it was during of his second tour. He had completed his first tour with No. 19 Sqn as an NCO then with a commission between April 1942 and December 1943 but did not make any claims during this tour. He made his first claim with 65 Sqn in a Mustang III on 17 September 1944. When he took command of 65, he was only 22 and was eventually awarded the DFC at the end of March. He remained with the RAF after the war and retired as a Group Captain in 1975. The pilot standing on his right, with the gloves, was Parke Smith, an American serving with the RAF (see the shoulder flash). *(via S. Brooking)*

D.W. Davis (RCAF) and W/O J.D. Howells, while the WingCo (on KH758) and Bradford claimed one each damaged as well. It seems that among the German pilots engaged were some Luftwaffe 'experten' as W/C Wickham and F/L 'Ham' Hamilton-Williams struggled fiercely against one without making any progress. Even the alleged turning qualities of the Mustang did not help get any advantage over the German. The squadron returned to base and two days later command was eventually given to one of the flight commanders, F/L J.D. Forster, who would lead 65 until the end of war. Only one more mission was carried out before the end of March, on the 30th, but it was uneventful.

The first operation in April was on the 2nd and, again, was an uneventful escort. The next mission came three days later and was an escort mission for Beaufighters on an anti-shipping strike to Bremanger. On 5 April 1945, in excellent visibility, the squadron's dozen Mustang IVs rendezvoused with the Dalachy Wing's Beaufighters and headed for the Norwegian coast. Two and a half hours later, as they were crossing the coast off Vaagso homeward bound, about fifteen Bf109s approached and were promptly engaged. Four of them were shot down. One fell to F/L Graham Pearson, in Mk IV KH695, for his second claim (the first having been made in a Mk.III during the previous February). F/O W.L. Black - RCAF - in KH642 also made his second claim with a 109 shot down while the new CO made his final claim, in KH788/YT-Q, he shot down a Me109. *He dived down and met one head on coming in to attack. He gave him a very short burst, and when he passed me he broke to starboard and got on his tail, closing from from 400 yards to 150 yards, firing 7-8 seconds burst.* Foster immediately observed strikes all round the cockpit and wing roots of the German aircraft and soon developed a rather severe glycol leak. Foster overshot and his No 2 saw him strike the water and disintegrate. F/L 'Maxie' Lloyd, flying KH685/YT-F, claimed one of the two probable 109s. This was his 5th and final claim on the Mustang.

Combat report:
F/O G. Pearson, 7 April 1945

FINAL INTELLIGENCE REPORT – (FORM F)

(Ref: Turnhouse Opflash No. 2 of 7.4.45)

Statistical

- A. Date. — 7th April, 1945.
- B. Sqdn. — 65 (East India) Sqdn.
- C. Type and Mark of A/C. — 4 Mustangs IV
- D. Time of Attack. — 1640 hours.
- E. Place of Attack. — 6113N 0600E
- F. Weather. — No cloud. Excellent visibility.
- G. Our Casualties – A/C — 1 Mustang IV missing.
- H. Our Casualties – Personnel. — F/Lt. Watt missing.
- J. Enemy Casualties in Air Combat. — 2 FW 190's destroyed. 1 FW 190 damaged.
- K. Nil.

General Report.

Close escort to a force of 24 Beaufighters was supplied by 12 Mustangs of 19 Sqdn while the 4 a/c of 65 Sqdn went ahead with an outrider when about 20 miles from the mouth of SOGNEFJORD. About 10 minutes after the Beaufighters had attacked 2 ships in VADHEIM FJORD a gaggle of 10 FW 190's approached at about 7000' from the South and our a/c dropped tanks and attacked.

PERSONAL COMBAT REPORT FOR F/Lt. PEARSON.
NO. 65/P   C.C.G. 65/P

I was flying Presto 3 detailed to look after one Beau outrider of a force of Beaus which attacked shipping in SOGNE FJORD. At about 1640 hours, ten minutes after the strike, a gaggle of e/a was reported by my No. 2, F/Lt. Romain, about 1500 ft. above us (i.e. 7500 ft.) 2000 yds behind. We immediately turned 180° starboard, the e/a which were 10-12 in number, flying in squadron formation, then dropped their tanks. I dived about 1000 ft. to gain speed and passed under their formation, pulled up and attacked the rear man of their port section, and noticed a number of strikes on his fuselage. My No. 2 meanwhile had broken to port and we became separated. The rest of the section scattered and the 190 in question flicked on to its back and dove straight down to the deck. I followed him down and was not followed by the remaining three of his section. The 190 went straight into a small valley and did steep turns between 0 - 100 ft. round several small log huts. I had a big advantage over him and got in several bursts from 200 - 50 yds with a number of strikes. There was a small flak gun in the vicinity which I was unable to locate as he only opened fire when my back was turned. After about 5 minutes of this another 190 came down and delivered a head-on attack but did not hit me. The original 190 by this time was blazing underneath and in a final ½ turn with him and more hits at close range, he crashed into the ground about 10 ft. below him and burst into flames. At this time the other 190 was about 1000 - 1500 yds down the valley east of me, about 150 ft. high and was obviously unable to see me and was jinking to north and south going away from me. I kept low on the ground, caught him up and fired at small deflection from about 350 yds about a 4 second burst. I noticed a few strikes on his fuselage; the pilot was either hit himself or panicked, for going round in a rate 2 turn to starboard, he flicked over to the port on to his back and plunged straight into the ground; the a/c exploded and was enveloped in a dense volume of thick black smoke. F/O Black saw the black smoke rising from the hill side shortly afterwards.

I claim 2 FW 190's destroyed.

Signed: Ges Pearson

No. 65 Squadron taxiing out to escort Coastal Command aircraft. The Mustang IVs are all equipped with long-range tanks. Note the fleet is a mix of camouflaged and natural metal finish aircraft.
(Andrew Thomas)

Two days later, No 19 Squadron from Peterhead provided a dozen Mustangs as close escort to a force of two dozen Beaufighters while four of 65's Mustangs pushed ahead. Soon after the strike aircraft had attacked two vessels in Vadheim Fjord about ten Fw190s appeared from the south. The Mustangs promptly dropped their underwing tanks and engaged. One of the pilots was F/L Graham Pearson, who was flying KH685, and claimed two of them as destroyed. This took his number of claims to five but, frustratingly, his fifth confirmed never came. Nonetheless, he would become the most successful pilot on the Mk.IV. At his side, F/O Black, flying as Number 4, also made his fifth claim when he damaged another of the Fw190s. Unfortunately F/Lt Watt was missing he was last heard in the target area calling up at about 1645 hours saying he had an enemy aircraft on his tail and he was also seen in a dog-fight with two Fw190s. One faint call which gave a bearingbut no fix led to intensive ASR search but without success. He actually survived and spent the rest of the war as a PoW. Two days later the squadron was detailed to provide an escort to anti-shipping Mosquitoes but returned home with nothing to report. However, on the 11th, S/L J.W. Foster was leading the squadron, together with twelve other Mustang IVs, from Peterhead to Porsgrund, Norway, as part of a fighter escort to 35 Mosquitos from the Banff Wing. F/L Frederick Hilley Bradford, at the head of his flight, was last seen leading his section while trying to protect the Mosquitos from a German fighter attack. Repeated calls on the R/T brought no response and F/L Bradford was posted missing with his Mustang IV KH685/YT-F. During this combat, 65 was able to claim two damaged aircraft (one 109 each for W/O Howells and F/L Simms) to compensate partially for this loss.

Until the end of the month, the unit was called upon to provide escort seven more times with the last being on the 24th. One Mustang was lost during that time, KH695/YT-E on 19th, which force-landed at Getterön on the west coast of Sweden after an engine failure during an escort mission over the Skagerrak for Banff Wing Mosquitos. F/L Graham Pearson who had four victories and a probable (all on Mustangs) was interned but, on his release, was awarded the DFC. Escort duty continued in May and, on the 3rd, twelve Mustang IVs took off at 16:45 to escort Beaufighters targeting the Kattegat. F/O Lucas had petrol leakage on the return flight and was forced to bail out 35 miles east of Newcastle in the North Sea. He was later picked up by ASR and returned to the squadron the next day which was the last day of war for the squadron. Indeed, war for 65 ended on 4 May when eight Mustangs, led by the CO, escorted Beaufighters on an anti-shipping mission to the Kattegat. By that time, the Mustangs on strength with the squadron were

JJust after VE-Day 65 Sqn exchanged its Mustangs with 122 Sqn. Foster chose KM148, still with the codes YT-Q, as his mount. *(via B. Brown)*

KH644, KH646, KH648, KH657, KH658, KH678, KH708, KH715, KH724, KH744, KH758, KH777, KH788, KH822, KH829, KM130 and KM223.

When the war ended, and before May was done, the unit switched with No. 122 Squadron and the Mustangs exchanged so, by mid-May, 65 would again fly, for a short time, a mixed force of MK.IIIs and Mk.IVs (eleven of the latter) as 122 had begun its conversion to the Mk.IV just after VE-Day. As with 19 Squadron, 65 moved a couple of times before being re-equipped with the Spitfire LF.16e in March 1946. The last Mustang IVs left in May. Accidents were rare during that time. However, on 14 June 1945, an odd accident occurred when, during a routine flight, a formation of four Mustang IVs were 'attacked' by two USAAF Mustangs and one of the American pilots, 1st Lt G.P. Barrett, struck the aircraft flown by F/O Colin Downes and caused serious damage and a temporary loss of control. Downes jettisoned the cockpit canopy, in preparation for bailing out, but regained control at the last moment and managed to return to base. The American pilot, who bailed out over the sea, was never found despite an extensive search. Also, F/Sgt A.C. Stoneley was killed, on 18 December 1945, while conducting an air test. At low level, he attempted an upward roll but applied too much back-pressure on the control column and the aircraft stalled and dived into the ground. Finally, 65 lost a Mustang IV during another air test, on 9 February 1946, when the aircraft swung on landing and the undercarriage collapsed. Fortunately, he pilot, F/L E.S. Hughes, escaped injuries.

Claims - 65 Squadron (Confirmed and Probable)

Date	Pilot	SN	Origin	Type	Serial	Code	Nb	Cat.
25.03.45	F/L Frederick H. **Bradford**	RAF No.119711	RAF	Fw190	**KH744**		1.0	C
	F/O Darrel W. **Davis**	Can./J.24593	RCAF	Fw190	**KH644**		1.0	C
	W/O James D. **Howells**	RAF No.1530990	RAF	Fw190	**KH657**		1.0	C
05.04.45	F/O William L. **Black**	Can./J.35794	RCAF	Bf109	**KH642**		1.0	C
	S/L John W. **Foster**	RAF No.134757	RAF	Bf109	**KH788**	YT-Q	1.0	C
	F/L Charles O.E. **Hamilton-Williams**	RAF No.88859	RAF	Bf109	**KH758**	YT-Z	1.0	C
	F/L John M.W. **Lloyd**	RAF No.139274	RAF	Bf109	**KH685**	YT-F	1.0	P
	F/L Graham S. **Pearson**	RAF No.127224	RAF	Bf109	**KH695**	YT-E	1.0	C
				Bf109			1.0	P
07.04.45	F/L Graham S. **Pearson**	RAF No.127224	RAF	Fw190	**KH685**	YT-F	2.0	C

Total: 11.0

Summary of the aircraft lost on Operations - 65 Squadron

Date	Pilot	S/N	Origin	Serial	Code	Fate
25.03.45	S/L Ian G. **Stewart**	RAF No.43983	RAF	**KH732**		†
11.04.45	F/L Frederick H. **Bradford**	RAF No.119711	RAF	**KH685**	YT-F	-
07.04.45	F/L Gordon C.L. **Watt**	RAF No.47448	RAF	**KH686**	YT-P	PoW
19.04.45	F/L Graham S. **Pearson**	RAF No.127224	RAF	**KH695**	YT-E	Int.
03.05.45	F/O John D. **Lucas**	RAF No.150488	RAF	**KH657**		-

Total: 5

Summary of the aircraft lost by accident - 65 Squadron

Date	Pilot	S/N	Origin	Serial	Code	Fate
14.06.45	F/O Colin B.W. **Downes**	RAF No.178290	RAF	**KM316**		-
18.12.45	F/Sgt Albert C. **Stonely**	RAF No.1805145	RAF	**KH707**		†
09.02.46	F/L Eric S. **Hughes**	RAF No.144000	RAF	**KM314**	YT-L	-

Total: 3

Graham Pearson ended the war in Sweden when he made an emergency landing there and was interned for just a couple of days. His aircraft, KH695/YT-E, is seen being dismantled. The spares would be used for the Swedish Mustangs which had been introduced into service two months earlier. *(Andrew Thomas)*

March 1945
August 1945

Victories - confirmed or probable claims: 7

First operational sortie:
23.03.45
Last operational sortie:
25.04.45

Number of sorties: 229

Total aircraft written-off: 6
Aircraft lost on operations: 2
Aircraft lost in accidents: 4

Squadron code letters:
FY

COMMANDING OFFICERS

S/L Dunham G. Seaton	RAF No.46705	RAF	...	10.07.45
S/L Paul C.P. Farnes	RAF No.88437	RAF	13.07.45	...

SQUADRON USAGE

A Spitfire squadron since the beginning of the war, No. 611 Squadron had switched to long-range escort missions from East Anglia in October 1944. The Mustang was seen as being more suitable for this task and it was obvious that a conversion of the squadron to this type would be for the better. When the first four Mustang IVs arrived, on the first day of March 1945, 611 was commanded by S/L Seaton. He was a former Army officer and had been in command since January. Soon after the squadron moved to Hundson to join other Mustang squadrons. In March, while still flying the Spitfire Mk.IX, conversion training was undertaken after operational duties were complete. By 15 March other Mustangs had been allocated and the squadron had become non-operational, in order to complete the transition which was achieved on 22 March. At that time, 611 had on

S/L Seaton (fifth from right), surrounded by other 611 pilots, talking to the Squadron's Intelligence Officer 'Spy' Tizzard (holding a note pad). It seems that Seaton did not participate in this op as he is not wearing flying clothing.

Mustang IV KH746/FY-R was on strength with 611 from the beginning of their time on Mustang IVs. The codes are not painted as per regulations as the individual letter and squadron code are painted on the same side of the roundel. That is why, upon arrival in the UK, the serial painted in the States behind the fuselage roundel was removed and repainted under the horizontal stabilisers. Note the KH746 partially erased by the weather conditions encountered over Western Europe during spring. No. 65 and 611 Sqns completed the same number of sorties with this mark, 229, which was also the highest number of sorties on type in Western Europe.
(B. Partridge via Andrew Thomas)

charge KH643, KH650, KH675, KH691, KH695, KH725, KH728, KH730, KH746, KH783, KH784, KH785, KH789, KH790, KH812 and KH844. The squadron became operational the next day and was airborne at 08:20 to protect a glider stream proceeding to the east of Wesel . The squadron patrolled for nearly five hours but the operation proved uneventful and they landed back at base at 13:00.

The first real test on Mustangs took place on 25 March (*Ramrod* 1515) when eleven Mustangs, led by the CO, were airborne at 07:25 to escort bombers to Hannover. This mission was uneventful. The next mission was organised two days later (*Ramrod* 1519) to escort 85 Lancasters over Hamm. Nothing was reported and on the return leg, after the bombers had been escorted to the Rhine, the squadron returned to sweep an area north of Hannover where railway trucks and a station were attacked as well as a village which was shot up and many strikes seen. Two more *Ramrods* were carried out before the end of March but only *Ramrod* 1523, on the 31st, was of interest as the squadron saw many Me262s attack the bomber stream but, although many attempts were made to intercept them, their speed made it impossible for the squadron to engage.

Reinforced by pilots from the recently disbanded No. 154 Squadron, 611 continued its operations during all of April. Fourteen *Ramrod* missions were carried out between the 3rd and the 25th and totaled 172 sorties. The squadron, however, had to wait until 16 April before any action really occurred. The squadron took off at 14:35, the WingCo Flying, Lt-Col Christie (Norwegian), flying with 611. The mission was to escort twenty Lancasters to Swinehausen then for the Mustangs, to sweep the Berlin area. After escorting the bombers to the target safely the squadron left for Berlin looking for enemy aircraft in the air. It proved a good move as plenty of enemy aircraft were soon seen. F/L Partridge first saw twenty of them flying below the squadron formation. They were identified as Fw190s and the squadron attacked without delay. The first to shoot one down was F/L 'Grousse' Partridge who fired a six second burst and observed strikes on the fuselage and port wing. The enemy aircraft dived towards the ground and was observed flaming. Partridge attacked another FW190 and he claimed it as damaged. Lt-Col Christie also attacked one of the Fw190s. He fired a five second burst at the leading aircraft in a formation of three from a range of 150 yards. He observed strikes on the port side of the engine and cockpit and also saw that the starboard wingtip had been damaged. The aircraft was then smoking badly and gliding straight ahead. He pulled out to the port side and made a second attack, opening up at 200 yards and closing to about 50 yards and dead astern. He fired several short bursts and saw strikes on the cockpit, engine and both wings. Then the port wing fell off

Two of the pilots who made a claim on the successful day of 16 April 1945. Ian Walker, left, claimed one probable Fw190 and, right, George Jones claimed two confirmed Fw190s. He would be awarded the DFC in August for his actions with 611.

and port wheel fell down. The German fighter did five or six quick rolls horizontally and crashed in flames in a wood. Other pilots of the squadron were also victorious that day. F/O G.A. Jones claimed two destroyed. He was dead astern of an enemy at about 280 yards and opened fire with a five second burst. He saw pieces flying past him and oil covered his windscreen. He then saw more strikes on the fuselage and the Fw190 burst into flames before diving and exploding upon hitting the ground in a nearby wood. Then he chased another Fw190 well below him and heading towards an airfield. He gave chase for three minutes until he was 200 yards astern. He fired a short burst but scored no hits so he fired another short burst. This time he saw strikes on the fuselage and mainplane so he continued to fire until the Fw190 began to disintegrate. Jones followed it down and saw it crash. At his side, W/O 'Kenny' Mack got another one while P/O G. Walker was unable to observe the results and could only claim a probably destroyed Fw190 as did P/O 'Tommy' Ward. In all, with five confirmed victories, two probables and one damaged, the 16th of April had been a very good day of the pilots of 611, not counting that F/L Partridge reported that they met up with Russian aircraft. They got close to them, at about 100 yards, waggled their wings, and the Russians waved to them too in response.

On 18 April Lt-Col Christie briefed the squadron on *Ramrod* 1544. Their task was to patrol enemy airfields in southern Denmark and northern Germany while Lancasters were bombing Heligoland. All were airborne at 12:30 and the squadron returned to base at 15.55 after an uneventful mission. Unfortunately, the WingCo Flying did not return. Christie's aircraft suffered an engine failure and caught fire and he was forced to bail out over enemy territory near Handorf and became a PoW for a short time. He was replaced by 'Jas' Storrar of No. 234 Squadron. On the 22nd the squadron was airborne again on Ramrod 1551 with twelve Mustangs, led by the CO, tasked to patrol a line from Cuxhaven to Zevern while Lancasters were bombing Bremen. At the end of the patrol F/L A.J. Grottick, who had been recently posted from No. 501 Squadron, developed engine trouble with his KH728 and was escorted by P/O Walker to the Allied lines where the situation became worse. Grottick chose to bail out over the Minden area. He landed safely and subsequent reports reported him being with a Canadian unit. Three days later the squadron conducted its last wartime operation, *Ramrod* 1554, but returned with nothing to report. The war ended and 611 moved to Scotland and was based at Peterhead until it disbanded on 15 August 1945. During this short period of time, routine flights were carried out and a couple of aircraft were lost in accidents. KH675, on 25 June, suffered an engine failure on take off followed by a belly landing. The pilot, W/O H.J. Thomas, was lucky to escape injury. On 9 July, KH784 also had engine trouble on take off and Pilot Officer D.T. Ward was slightly injured. A little more than a week later, on 18 July, KH643 stalled while attempting to overshoot a truck on the runway but ended up colliding with it. Again, the pilot's luck held and F/L J.L.W. Innes survived unscathed. Six days before disbandment, the last Mustang IV was wrecked when W/O D.L. McNeil (RAAF) overshot the runway while returning from a practice flight. The flaps could not be lowered due to a leak in the hydraulics system. The aircraft was damaged but no repairs were undertaken, as the RAF had enough aircraft on spare, and it was eventually converted to components .

Claims - 611 Squadron (Confirmed and Probable)

Date	Pilot	SN	Origin	Type	Serial	Code	Nb	Cat.
16.04.45	Lt-Col Werner **Christie**	N.1071	RNoAF	Fw190	**KH790**	WHC	1.0	C
	F/O Georges A. **Jones**	RAF No.148894	RAF	Fw190	**KM150**		2.0	C
	W/O Kenneth C. **Mack**	RAF No.1443565	RAF	Fw190	**KH645**		1.0	C
	F/L Brian L. **Partridge**	RAF No.150052	RAF	Fw190	**KH730**		1.0	C
	P/O Ian G. **Walker**	RAF No.188562	RAF	Fw190	**KH884**		1.0	P
	P/O Tom **Ward**	RAF No.188545	RAF	Fw190	**KH650**		1.0	P

Total: 7.0

Summary of the aircraft lost on Operations - 611 Squadron

Date	Pilot	S/N	Origin	Serial	Code	Fate
18.04.45	Lt-Col Werner **Christie**	N.1071	RNoAF	**KH790**	WHC	**PoW**
22.04.45	F/L Albert J. **Grottick**	RAF No.136572	RAF	**KH728**		-

Total: 2

No. 611 Sqn lost two Mustang IVs on operations but, fortunately, both pilots survived. Right: Werner Christie was a major personality in the RNoAF and an ace with ten confirmed victories (one being shared). He spent the last weeks of the war as a PoW. After the war he continued his career with the RNoAF and retired as a Major General. He had arrived at Hundson on 8 March to lead the Wing comprising Nos. 154 and 611 Sqns, the first fully equipped Mustang IV units. Left: 'Jimmy' Grottick was also an experienced pilot with one confirmed victory and two V-1s destroyed claimed while serving with No. 501 Sqn.

Summary of the aircraft lost by accident - 611 Squadron

Date	Pilot	S/N	Origin	Serial	Code	Fate
25.06.45	W/O Henry J. **Thomas**	RAF No.1393986	RAF	**KH675**		-
09.07.45	P/O Tom **Ward**	RAF No.188545	RAF	**KH784**		-
14.07.45	F/L John L.W. **Innes**	RAF No.120945	RAF	**KH643**		-
09.08.45	W/O David L. **McNeil**	Aus.414815	RAAF	**KH647**		-

OTHER FIGHTER SQUADRONS

No. 19 Squadron (code QV):

After over one year of operations on Mustangs, and close to 3,400 sorties completed on the Mk.III, No. 19 Squadron received its first Mustang Mk.IVs in the last days of March, and training was quickly undertaken between the 31 March and 2 April. Among the Mk.IVs received were KH655/QV-P, KH674, KH695, KH698/QV-Q, KH739, KH742/QV-A, KH756, KH761/QV-T, KH778, KH818/QV-F, KH847/QV-U and KM137. Until the end of the war the squadron would fly almost exclusively on this type while keeping a handful of Mk.IIIs on hand at least until the end of April. Squadron Leader Hearne had been in charge since December 1944. The squadron's main task was to provide escort to Coastal Command aircraft. Hearne had served with No. 65 Squadron for a long time, and had good experience on Mustangs, when he was posted in to 19 Squadron. Despite the arrival of the more popular Mk.IV on strength, the CO surprisingly decided at first to keep his Mk.III (KH511/QV-J). The first main operation of the month was carried out on the 3rd and was the escort of 32 Beaufighters to Egersund in Norway. However, bad weather prevented any strikes and the Mustangs returned home safely after 3.5 hours in the air. The next day, while the squadron was released, they were called upon to escort Beaufighters once more. The unit was able to gather together twelve pilots and the mission was executed without incident while the Beaufighters claimed a damaged 3,000 ton merchant vessel. Another escort, for Mosquitos this time, was flown on the 5th. Some light arms fire was encountered on the way back over the Danish coast and, just as the squadron was crossing out, F/L James Butler in KM137, leading White section, was seen to pull up, burst into flames and go straight into the sea a mere 100 yards off the coast. No movement was seen and he was presumed to have been killed. The squadron flew again on the 7th and the 9th. Both escort operations were uneventful as far as the Mustangs were concerned. Another Beaufighter escort was performed on the 11th with the Coastal Command aircraft leaving a 3,000 ton merchant vessel sinking. Afterwards Hearne, in his Mk.III, led the squadron eastward to sweep around Lister at 5,000 feet until they came to Fede Fjord. Hearne sighted four Bf109s over Lister airfield. Chasing after one of them, he shot down the Staffelführer of 16./JG5, Ltn Adolf Gillet, some three miles from the airfield. The German pilot was wounded but did not survive despite being rescued by Norwegian fishermen. The next success for Hearne came soon after this one during an escort to eighteen Beaufighters on the 14th. Hearne was the only pilot to score in April, making him an ace on Mustangs but only on Mk.IIIs, then numbering only three or four on strength by that time, as he made no claim while flying a Mk.IV. Five more escorts were provided by the end of the month with the last being on the 26th. That day the Mustangs dissuaded about 25 Bf109s from attacking the Beaufighters by flying close to them. Even if no combat was recorded, the goal of the escort duty, to prevent any enemy attack, was achieved. Now fully equipped with Mk.IVs, the squadron continued its escort job in the first days of May. The aircraft on hand were KH655, KH867, KH664, KH674, KH698, KH742, KH756, KH778, KH818, KH847, KH867/QV-S, KH858, KM108, KM118/QV-X, KM152/QV-W, KM193/QV-J (the CO's new mount) and KM272/QV-Y. The squadron was airborne on the 2nd with twelve aircraft, on the 3rd with twelve again and on the 4th with six aircraft. Sadly it was during this last mission, during which an E-boat was sunk by the Mosquitos, that two Mustangs from the squadron collided and crashed into the sea. The two pilots, F/L J. Davidson and P/O B.M. Matta (RNZAF) were killed. Two other pilots, F/O Scholfield and F/L Yearwood were also hit by flak but returned to base with minor damage. In all, the squadron flew 136 sorties on Mk.IVs but did not score and lost three aircraft on operations. The unit continued to operate the Mustang Mk.IV until March 1946, being located

Summary of the aircraft lost on Operations - 19 Squadron

Date	Pilot	S/N	Origin	Serial	Code	Fate
05.04.45	F/L James **Butler**	RAF No.136573	RAF	**KM137**		†
04.05.45	F/L Joseph **Davidson**	RAF No.127915	RAF	**KH818**	QV-F	†
	P/O Basil M. **Natta**	NZ422308	RNZAF	**KH674**		†

Total: 3

at Acklington, north of Newcastle, by the end of May before moving south in August to Bradwell Bay, located north of Southend. A last move to Molesworth (north of Bedford) occurred the following month before the Mustangs were replaced with Spitfire LF.16s. During that time, only one Mustang was lost in an accident. On 20 June 1945, having taken off as No. 2 of three aircraft to look at the weather, the formation was soon caught by poor weather with a cloud base of only 500 feet. The leader of the formation, F/L Shirreff, decided to return to base. While doing so, the three aircraft encountered a bank of mist and the leader called for each pilot to climb above the cloud individually so they could rejoin. F/L R.W. Robson was the only one not to do so and was killed in the crash.

Summary of the aircraft lost by accident - 19 Squadron

Date	Pilot	S/N	Origin	Serial	Code	Fate
20.06.45	F/L Robert W. **Robson**	RAF No.49208	RAF	**KH664**		†

Total: 1

Squadron Leader Hearne (third from left) with members of 19 Squadron. *(via S. Brooking)*

Mustang KH655/QV-P in flight while escorting Coastal Command aircraft. For this the Mustangs needed long-range fuel tanks which were used during the inbound leg. This aircraft was usually flown by F/O Edward R. Davies who was with 19 Sqn since May 1944.
The colour of the nose and spinner are not known with certain but the various photographic evidence available suggests white and blue - see also KH818/QV-F below - , (and not yellow-back) which was similar to the colours used by the squadron in the inter-war period. After the war, the Squadron re-introduced the blue/white check markings around the nose of its aircraft. *(below ww2.images.com)*

No. 122 Squadron (code MT):

As mentioned for the 65 Squadron, an exchange of aircraft occurred shortly after VE-Day. At the end of April, the 122 had begun to receive its first Mk.IV, like KM148, KM165, KM192, KM255, KM261, KM273, KM276 and KM287. Flying on Mustang Mk.IIIs since February 1944, the squadron was commanded by S/L John A.G. Jackson who had been awarded the DFC in August 1944 while flying with 66 Sqn on Spitfires. Taking command of the 122 in February 1945, he would lead the squadron until its re-equipment on Spitfires in August 1945. Two Mustangs were lost during this short period, KH644, four days after the end of war in Europe. Despite the aircraft having an unserviceable radio, it was flown by F/O Robert H. Casburn[2] from San Fransisco, California (USA), on a general handling sortie. The aircraft was seen flying at 1,000 feet when it entered a vertical dive from which it did not recover. The pilot had no chance to survice the crash. The reason for the dive was never established. Shortly before leaving the Mustangs for the Spitfire, another dramatic accidnet occurred, on 3 August. Returning from a routine sortie, F/L Douglas Gihl landed too fast and too far along the runway. The aircraft ren off the end and struck a fence before turning over. It seems that it took too much time to lift the aircraft to save Gihl who died in the aircraft of his injuries sustained during the crash. The Mustangs IVs known to have used by the squadron were: KH646, KH658, KH708, KH715, KH724, KH744, KH754, KH758, KH777, KH788, KH822, KH829, KM130 (all ex-65 Sqn), later joined by KH641, KH655, KH747, KM132.

Summary of the aircraft lost by accident - 122 Squadron

Date	Pilot	S/N	Origin	Serial	Code	Fate
12.05.45	F/O Robert H. **Casburn**	RAF No.162938	(US)/RAF	**KH644**		†
03.08.45	F/L Douglas E. **Gihl**	RAF No.138098	RAF	**KH829**		†
		Total: 2				

No. 126 Squadron (code 5J):

No. 126 Squadron was a Mustang unit from December 1944 and carried out operations with the Mk.III until the end of the war. In August 1945, when No. 234 Squadron converted to Spitfires, it passed its Mk.IVs to 124 and these were used until its turn to convert to Spitfires came in March 1946. The following Mustang IVs are known to have served with 126: KH641, KH649, KH696, KH712, KH729, KH765, KH843, KH857, KH863, KM103, KM114, KM125, KM128, KM134, KM172, KM203, KM251, KM279 and KM299 (all ex-234).

No. 154 Squadron (code HG):

No. 154 Squadron was formed in November 1941 and one year later was sent to the Middle East. Disbanded in France at the end of October 1944, it was re-formed in the UK at Biggin Hill two weeks later and received ageing Spitfire Mk.VIIs. The squadron was placed under the responsibility of S/L G. Stonhill. It became operational in mid-January 1945 but very few missions were actually carried out with the Spitfires before the squadron converted to the Mustang Mk.IV. It became the first unit to fly exclusively on this mark before the end of the war. The first Mk.IV arrived at the squadron on the morning of 3 February and during that month operational duties were carried out with the Spitfires while training continued on the Mustangs. The aircraft allocated were KH641 (the first Mustang Mk.IV), KH647, KH651, KH659, KH665, KH666, KH668, KH670, KH680, KH694, KH697, KH700, KH709, KH711, KH721, KH729, KH735, KH737 and KH764. The squadron was then united with 611 Squadron, also equipped with Mustang Mk.IVs, to form the Hundson Wing which was placed under the leadership of Norwegian ace Lt-Col Werner Christie. He had been awarded the DFC while flying with the Norwegian No. 332 Squadron.

The war began for the squadron's Mustangs on 9 March when the CO took off with the squadron at 12:35 to escort Lancasters detailed to bomb Relinghausen. However, the CO had to return early owing to trouble with his canopy and F/L Andrew, the B Flight CO, took command of the formation. The squadron returned safely to base, after four hours of flight, with nothing to report. The following day another escort mission was tasked to the squadron and also proved to be uneventful. This was followed by further escort missions on the 11th (led by Lt-Col Christie) and the 12th. During the latter the squadron suffered its first loss on Mustangs when the B Flight leader, F/L E. Andrew had to bale out over the target owing to engine trouble and became a PoW. He had flown with 17, 229 & 64 Squadron before joining 154 Squadron in November 1944. On the 13th the squadron carried out its first sweep but no German aircraft were seen. It then participated in nine more escort missions up to the 26th. All were uneventful and each flight lasted between four and five hours. On the 27th the squadron was dispatched to escort Lancasters to Hamm and were again led by Lt-Col Christie. The escort component of the operation was uneventful but, after its successful completion, the squadron returned to sweep Lubeck where enemy fighters were seen. In the ensuing melee, the WingCo claimed two Fw190s destroyed and one more damaged while W/O V.A. Bunting claimed a probable. F/L N. Lee (a third-tour pilot who had earned a DFC over Malta in 1942) and P/O R.A. Todd shared one Fw190 claimed as damaged. No loss was reported by the squadron. No operation was flown on the 28th but and on the 29th the squadron was again called to provide escorts for Lancasters bombing Hallendorf (led by the CO this time). Rendezvous was made as planned but, fifteen minutes before reaching the target, the squadron was ordered to return to base. W/O Standrin peeled off just before this order and was therefore posted missing. Alongside this bad news, pilots and personnel had been told that the squadron would be disbanded once more at the end of the month after completion of its last operation. That day the squadron took off at 06:50, led by the CO, to provide an escort to Lancasters bombing Hamburg. Some Me262s were seen to attack the bombers but their speed made it impossible to engage them. Despite this the CO shot one long burst but the distance was such that he could not expect any success or see any results. F/Sgt J.C Gilbertson-Pritchard was heard to say he was short of oxygen and became separated from the rest of the squadron. Later, a Mustang was seen to dive into the sea 1-2 miles off Lowestoft. It was believed that Pritchard was still on board when the Mustang hit the water. Over the next few days, while the war was over for 154, the pilots continued flying and all were dispersed to other operational squadrons. The squadron completed 213 sorties on Mustangs in one month of operations.

Claims - 154 Squadron (Confirmed and Probable)

Date	Pilot	SN	Origin	Type	Serial	Code	Nb	Cat.
27.03.45	Lt-Col Werner **Christie**	N.1071	RNoAF	Fw190	**KH790**	WHC	2.0	C
	W/O Vincent A. **Bunting**	RAF No.1259311	RAF	Fw190		HG-W	1.0	P
		Total: 3.0						

Mustang KH765/HG-R was regularly flown by F/L Norman Lee, one of the squadron's aces who distinguished himself over Malta with No. 229 Sqn and was awarded the DFC. The letter 'R' was painted in red while the squadron code letters were black. *(E. Andrew via Andrew Thomas)*

Summary of the aircraft lost on Operations - 154 Squadron

Date	Pilot	S/N	Origin	Serial	Code	Fate
12.03.45	F/L Edward **Andrews**	RAF No.61498	RAF	**KH721**	HG-A	**PoW**
29.03.45	W/O Arthur **Standrin**	RAF No.106443	RAF	**KH697**	HG-K	†
	F/Sgt John C. **Gilbertson-Pritchard**	RAF No.1084862	RNZAF	**KH651**	HG-P	†

Total: 3

No. 234 Squadron (code AZ):

Based at Bentwaters from December 1944, north of Ipswich, 234 had been flying Mustang IIIs since October 1944. Placed under the command of S/L J.E. Storrar, a very experienced pilot and an ace who had been in the breach since 1939. The squadron's task was long-range escort to the bomber squadrons flying deeply into Germany by day. The squadron exchanged its Mk.IIIs for brand new Mk.IVs on the first day of April (KH707, KH712, KH843, KH857, KH860, KM103, KM114, KM125, KM128, KM134, KM203, KM251, KM279, KM299 and KM305) but kept a couple of Mk.IIIs on hand and they would fly side by side with the new Mk.IVs during the first missions of April. The squadron had the opportunity to use their new aircraft for the first time on 3 April. Airborne at 14:10, and led by Storrar, the squadron provided an escort for 250 Lancasters bombing Nordhausen (*Ramrod* 1527). The escort was carried out according to plan and the squadron returned to base, after more than 4.5 hours flying, without any loss or claim to report. Another escort was carried out the next day - the uneventful *Ramrod* 1528 - before the squadron was released for several days to undertake a training program. Operations resumed on the 9th with *Ramrod* 1533 (involving 64 and 126 Sqn on Mk.IIIs) and the escort of fifty Lancasters bombing oil-storage tanks at Hamburg. Just after leaving the target, enemy aircraft were reported and the squadron, then at 26,000 feet, turned in behind the bombers. About twenty Me262s were sighted and engagement attempted. However, as the Mustangs were at extreme gun range, no results or hits were reported. The Me262s, however, did their job well as one Lancaster was seen blowing up as a result of enemy action. The next day the squadron escorted 200 Lancasters to Leipzig (*Ramrod* 1535) without incident. Ramrod missions continued during April but no opportunity was given to the pilots to make any claims. On the 20th the CO was promoted WingCo Flying of the Hundson wing following the loss of W/C Christie two days previously. Storrar led the squadron for the last time on *Ramrod* 1547 to Regensburg. The command of the squadron was given to F/L Peter Steib, formerly of No. 122 Squadron (another Mustang unit). However, as he was still on a course at the Fighter Leaders School, he would not arrive at the squadron until the 27th. By that time, 234 had carried out its last mission for April two days before over Berchtesgaden. On the 30th the squadron moved to Peterhead where its final wartime operations would be carried out, in support of Coastal Command aircraft this time, as the war was over for Bomber Command by the early days of May 1945. On the 3rd, the squadron, led by Steib, took off in company with No. 19 Squadron with W/C Wickham leading the two squadrons, on an escort of Mosquitos on a shipping strike south of the Kattegat in Denmark. All of the aircraft returned safely to base after 4.6 hours of flight. The mission was repeated the next day and, after 2.5 hours, a convoy of three merchant vessels and two destroyers was found and attacked by the Mosquitos. All of the ships were damaged. Fifteen minutes later, just after crossing over the Danish coast, P/O 'Pete' Bell called up to say that he had been hit in the arm. The CO suggested that he fly as far south as possible in the hope of reaching the British 2nd Army progressing north from the south of Denmark. However this proved impossible for Bell and he had to crash land behind enemy lines where he became a PoW for a couple of days before being repatriated ten

In the breech since 1939, 'Jas' Storrar became the WingCo Flying of the Hundson Wing, when Lt-Col Christie was shot down and taken prisoner, after having led 234 Sqn on Mustangs since January 1945. With 14 confirmed victories (two being shared), Storrar made his claims on Hurricanes and Spitfires but did not have the chance to increase his score while flying Mustangs.

Mustang KM232/JAS with which 'Jas' Storrar flew his last operations. As with many WingCo leaders, he was authorised to paint his initials as codes. He had, however, already taken this liberty when he was a Squadron Leader! *(Andrew Thomas)*

days later. This operation became the last mission of the war for the squadron. In a short time it had completed 163 sorties on the Mustang IV. Flying continued in May but without the long-range tanks aerobatics were possible and the pilots enjoyed throwing their aircraft around the sky. On the 23rd and 31st the squadron was called upon to participate in an ASR search for a missing aircraft. This was the last significant event before the squadron exchanged its Mustangs for Spitfire Mk.IXs in August. The last flights were carried out on the 7th and the same day all Mustangs were handed over to No. 126 Squadron.

Summary of the aircraft lost on Operations - 234 Squadron

Date	Pilot	S/N	Origin	Serial	Code	Fate
04.05.45	P/O Peter J.W. BELL	RAF No.184700	RAF	**KH860**	AZ-G	**PoW**

Total: 1

Mustang KH860/AZ-G in which P/O Bell failed to return from a shipping strike off the Danish islands on 4 May 1945. Bell was slightly wounded by flak and became a PoW for a couple of days (or a few hours!).
(R.T. Williams via A. Thomas)

Mustang IV KM220 during the early phases of the usage of the type in April 1945 at Andrews Field. KM220 is wearing the wartime codes 'RF' which were changed to 'PD' in August 1945.
(Wilhelm Ratuszynski)

No. 303 (Polish) Squadron (code RF then PD):

Up to April 1945, the 303 had been a Spitfire squadron, based at Coltishall. In spring 1945, the squadron was selected to transition on the Mustang to carry out escort missions. The 303 was not the first Polish fighter squadron to be equipped with the Mustang, the Poles being among the very first to receive the Mk.III at the beginning of 1944, but the 303 would become the only Polish squadron to be fully equipped with the Mk.IV.

The 303 made a move to Andrews Field early in April, where other Polish Mustang squadrons were stationed (306, 309, 315), the last Polish Mustang squadron, the 316 being at Coltishall. The first Mk.IVs were soon received (KH663, KH769, KH825, KH836, KH855, KH866, KH868, KM102, KM112, KM113, KM209, KM220, KM239, KM263) and training commenced at once intensively, helped with a couple of old Mustang Mk.Is to ease the transition. Before the month was dead, the squadron had become operational, over 350 hours being logged for the month, for the loss of a single Mustang Mk.IV, KH855 on 28 April, which swung on take-off and hitting a tractor parked on the hedge. The pilot, F/O Krol, escaped injuries. In the meantime, the squadron had carried its first mission on Mustang, *Ramrod* 1552 (escort for 150 Lancaster to Flesburg) on the 23rd, led by the S/L Dobrinski, the CO, in collaboration with No. 316 (Polish) and 122 Squadrons. Take-of took place at 16.15, ten aircraft being airborne with a couple of minutes, but after half and hour of flight, F/Sgt Michalak (KM263) and P/O Nowinski (KM220) had to return to base owing technical trouble. The mission was uneventful, all the remaining eight aircraft touching ground at 21.00. Two days later, the squadron took off for the last time for a war flight, another *Ramrod* (No. 1554), an escort mission of 250 Lancaster to Berchesgarden, which was uneventful. The 303 completed in 16 sorties on Mustang.

S/L Boleslaw Drobinski (middle), one of the Polish aces of the RAF, became the last wartime CO of the most famous Polish fighter squadron in the RAF and was therefore responsible for 303 Sqn becoming operational on the Mustang. He eventually relinquished his command, in January 1946, to S/L Witold Lokuciewski (on his right). Lokuciewski, who was one of the original members of 303, had returned from captivity as he was shot down in March 1942. He participated in the Great Escape but was re-captured and was lucky not to be executed. After the war Lokuciewski returned to Poland and became the military attaché in London between 1968 and 1972. Drobinski chose to settle in Great Britain. The other pilots in this photo are F/L Kazimierz Budzik (first from left) and, on Dobrinski's left, F/L Stanislaw Zdanowski (B Flight CO) and F/L Marian Szleskowski (A Flight)
(Wilhelm Ratuszynski)

25

The 303 did not participate to the occupation of Germany, and remained in UK until it was disbanded on 11 December 1946. All flight had ceased already since the 26 November. Between VE-Day and November 1946, the 303 logged 4500 hours of light, and the 303 knew a rather high attrition rate loss, five Mustangs were lost in accident during that time. The first accident occurred on 20 August, when KM113 collided with KM201 whilst coming out from cloud. None of the two pilots survived. The second accident cost the life of F/O J. Schandler on 2 January 1946, when his aircraft stalled on take-off, hit the ground and exploded, while about one week later, W/O Lubinski swung on landing returning from a formation flight, leading his Mustang to the scrapyard. Two weeks later, KH744 was badly damaged in a ground collision with KH868, but the pilots escaped injuries. Then, on 29 March, 1946 when the engine of KH747 failed on take-off at the height of 300 feet; the pilot, W/O K. Sztuka tried to make a U-turn, but the speed was too low and the aircraft stalled to the ground bringing the pilot to his death. Two months later, it was the turn of KM102 to be lost when its pilot, F/O T. Haczkiewicz lost consciousness while flying above the North Sea. Fortunately, the pilot was able to recover in time, but not enough however as the Mustang touched the water obliging the pilot to make a ditching. All things considered, the 303 had the worst peace safety record on that type. The 303 had in charge in the days of its existence, the following Mustang IV: KH663/PD-L, KH669/PD-P KH754, KH770/PD-Y, KH825/PD-C, KH868, KM112/PD-D, KM115/PD-V, KM237/PD-R, KM186/PD-A, KM191, KM220, KM226, KM239, KM297/PD-K.

Summary of the aircraft lost by accident - 303 (Polish) Squadron

Date	Pilot	S/N	Origin	Serial	Code	Fate
28.04.45	F/O Julian **Krok**	P-2419	PAF	**KH855**	RF-A	-
20.08.45	W/O Alojzy **Rutecki**	P.780703	PAF	**KM113**		†
	F/Sgt Stanisław **Magdziak**	P.782139	PAF	**KM201**		†
02.01.46	F/O Jan **Schandler**	P-2428	PAF	**KH836**		†
11.01.46	W/O Wacław **Łubieński**	P.794657	PAF	**KM238**		-
25.01.46	F/L Tadeusz **Sikorski**	P-2352	PAF	**KH744**		-
29.03.46	W/O Konrad **Sztuka**	P.704334	PAF	**KH747**		†
08.05.46	F/O Tadeusz **Haczkiewicz**	P-2311	PAF	**KM102**		-

Total: 8

The last CO's Mustang, KM112/PD-D, with the new squadron codes as applied from August 1945. Lokuciewski has painted his tally under the cockpit, eleven swastikas, but his official score from September 1939 in Poland to March 1942 in the UK is established as 10 confirmed victories, one being shared, and four probables.

No. 442 (RCAF) Squadron (code Y2):

442 Sqn was among the last three RCAF overseas squadrons to be formed. It was first equipped with Spitfires and within the 2 TAF participated to the liberation of Europe. In March 1945, it was operated from the Netherlands under the command of S/L Mitchell 'Johnny' Johnston. The last mission on Spitfire was carried out on 17th and the following day the squadron moved to the UK leaving its Spitfires on the Continent. After leave, it began to reassemble at Hundson on 1 April to convert on Mustang Mk.IV, the aircraft taken on charge being KH641, KH647/Y2-H, KH659/Y2-I, KH665/Y2-V, KH666/Y2-P, KH668/Y2-T, KH680/Y2-B, KH694/Y2-P, KH700/Y2-S, KH709/Y2-J, KH711/Y2-N, KH729/Y2-A, KH735/Y2-W, KH737/Y2-D, KM122/Y2-F and KM218/Y2-Q. Most were former 154 Squadron machines. The first week was dedicated to the conversion at such which was swift and uneventful, and 175 hours flown. On the 9th, the 442 flew in operation for the first time with its Mustang Mk.IVs, the WinCo Flying of Hundson Wing – Lt Col W.H. Christie – flying with squadron for this special occasion. This mission, an escort to Lancasters with target of Hamburg was uneventful, and on the completion of the escort duty, the 442 went on sweep over Flensburg area, here too uneventful, the aircraft returning to base after five hours of flight. Escort missions were provided to Bomber Command bombers, on the 10th, 11th and 13th with no incident to report, and again on 15th, but this time, the squadron had to record its first loss, when F/L John N.G. Dick was posted missing from an escort mission of Lancaster to Swinemunde. He was last heard when the squadron was turning back for home. The next day, he was a kind of revenge. That day, the 442 had taken off for another escort - same target as the previous day. The escort was uneventful as such, and the squadron proceed to sweep the NE of Berlin area in hazy weather. There, they bounced some Fw190s and during the 15-minutes fight that followed three claims were made. F/O Wilson chased one of them with his wingman, F/O 'Rocky' Robillard. Robillard gave a short burst and strikes were seen, but he got out of position to continue the combat. Wilson was about 1000 yards away, closing rapidly to 250 yards and he gave the fighter a two-second burst with five-tenths degree deflection. He saw the enemy caught fire and crashed into a small wood and exploded. The claim was shared by both pilot, while F/L Shenk, claimed one more as probable; Shenck was an American who had flown with the Eagle squadrons a couple of years before (with No. 121 Sqn between July and December 1941). Another uneventful escort was carried out on the 18th, followed by another the next day, but two planes crashed, the first flown by F/O Robillard who lost control on take-off, the pilot escaping

Mustang IV KH661/Y2-C participated in 442's last operation, on 9 May over the Channel Islands, with F/O P. Bremner as pilot. Note the overseas roundel.
(Bill Coffman)

Mustang IV KH661/Y2-H was also one of the thirteen aircraft on that final op of 9 May led by W/C Storrar. Its pilot was F/L K.K. Charman. This aircraft had the distinction in sharing in the destruction of an Fw190 on 16 April when flown by F/O Wilson. Note the unusual way the individual letter and squadron codes are applied with both ahead of the fuselage roundel even though the Mustang to the left in natural metal finish seems to follow the regulations. In the background, Y2-A, the CO's mount, (see colour profile) and 'JAS', the WingCo's aircraft, can be seen. *(via A. Thomas)*

injuries but the Mustang was good for scrap and F/O D.J. Jeffrey had to belly land its Mustang (KM122), at Cateburry due to engine trouble without major consequences for the pilot and the plane. Four more escort missions were flown during the next days, the last on the 24th, the new WinCo flying, W/C Storrar flying withe 442 for this occasion. The escort was provided to Lancaster to Berchesgarden, nothing special had to be reported. It was the last of the 134 escort sorties recorded over Germany and over 500 operational hours had been logged. However, the 442 was called a last time on 9 May top participate to the liberation of the Channel Islands, 14 Mustangs patrolling in the area during over 2.5 hours with nothing to report , the W/C Storrar flying with the 442 once more.

During the next months until disbandment little flying was done, the squadron having not been selected to participate to the occupation of Germany, but that did not prevented fatal accident. Two days after VE-Day, W/O Henry S. Lorenz undertook an authorized low level flying sortie when he attempted to carry out a double roll from an height of 100 feet, a height which not enough to complete the manoeuvre safely and the Mustang hit the ground killing the pilot instantly. One month later, F/O Vernon McClung, in the aim to try its machine to its maximum of the capacities, initiated a dive at over 450 mph, the maximum allowed. However, an ammunition panel came off and the aircraft broke up in the dive, crashing into the sea off Portland Bay. When the last engine shut down the 442 could be proud to have logged 1700 hours on Mustangs.

Claims - 442 (RCAF) Squadron (Confirmed and Probable)

Date	Pilot	SN	Origin	Type	Serial	Code	Nb	Cat.
16.04.45	F/O Leonard H. **Wilson**	Can./J.37856	RCAF	Fw190	**KH647**	Y2-H	0.5	C
	F/O Roger J. **Robillard**	Can./J.28182	RCAF		**KH668**	Y2-T	0.5	C
	F/L Warren V. **Shenk**	Can./J.15072	(us)/RCAF	Fw190	**KH659**	Y2-I	1.0	P
	Total: 2.0							

Mustang IV KH668/Y2-T in which F/O Robillard shared the destruction of an Fw190 on 16 April 1945. However it was F/O 'Art' Nowlan who was flying this machine for the squadron's final operation of the war on 9 May. Behind is KH747/Y2-Y with the codes and individual letters also painted ahead of the roundel but with the 'Y2' preceding the 'Y' and, therefore, the total opposite of Y2-T! *(Bill Coffman)*

Summary of the aircraft lost on Operations - 442 (RCAF) Squadron

Date	Pilot	S/N	Origin	Serial	Code	Fate
15.04.45	F/L John N. G. **Dick**	Can./J.21907	RCAF	**KH764**		†
19.04.45	F/O Roger J. **Robillard**	Can./J.28182	RCAF	**KH666**	Y2-P	-

Total: 2

Mustang IV KH680/Y2C 'Edmonton Special' also participated in 442's last op on 9 May with P/O A.J. Mallandaine at the controls. *(Bill Coffman)*

Summary of the aircraft lost by accident - 442 (RCAF) Squadron

Date	Pilot	S/N	Origin	Serial	Code	Fate
10.05.45	WO1 Sylvester H. **Lorenz**	Can./R.112257	RCAF	**KH665**	Y2-V	†
18.06.45	F/O Vernon F. **McClung**	Can./J.37017	RCAF	**KH666**	Y2-P	†

Total: 2

WITH OTHER UNITS IN WESTERN EUROPE

From the beginning of the introduction of the Mustang into the operational squadrons, the WingCo Flying of Mustang wings quickly selected the Mk.IV and their aircraft appear in the various Station Flight inventories during the last stages of the war and after. In Europe, besides W/C Storrar's aircraft (KM232/JAS) and W/C Christie's (KH790/WHC) already mentioned, W/C J.B. Wray, who took over Storrar's position in August 1945, repainted KM232 with 'JBW'. This aircraft would be lost the following 14 November when W/C Derek R. Walker borrowed it to fly to Heston, London. Bad weather forced him to re-route to Hendon where the controller refused him permission to land. While approaching Hendon airfield the Mustang crashed into houses nearby and Walker was killed instantly. Walker had joined the RAF before the war and had fought over the Mediterranean first on Blenheim IFs with No. 30 Squadron then with Nos. 127 and 260 Squadrons on Hurricanes before eventually returning to the UK where he flew Typhoons. W/C P.R.C. Wickham used, as WingCo Flying of the Peterhead Wing, one Mustang (KM237/PW) late in the war. 'Mike' Donnet, a Belgian pilot, also flew a Mustang while WingCo Flying of the Bentwaters Wing. He flew a couple of sorties on KM121/MLD before suffering an accident in this aircraft on 23 April 1945 when he belly landed after an engine failure on take off for a ferry flight.

Two Mustang leaders. Left, Peter Wickham, a pre-war RAF pilot who started the war in the Mediterranean with Nos. 33 and 112 Sqns before returning to the UK where he commanded Nos. 131 and 122 Sqns. He then led No. 122 Wing of 2 TAF. In March 1945, he became the Wing Leader of the Peterhead Wing. He continued his career with the RAF after the war and retired as a Group Captain. Left, Michel 'Mike' Donnet, a pre-war Belgian military pilot who was a PoW in May 1940 and was released in January 1941. He fled Belgium in July 1941 in a hidden Stampe SV-4 and joined the RAF. He became operational in September with No. 64 Sqn. By March 1944 he was the OC of No. 350 (Belgian) Squadron then, in October '44, the WingCo Flying of the Hawkinge Wing before taking command, in February 1945, of the Bentwaters Wing. He continued his career with the new Belgian Air Force and retired as a Lieutenant-General in 1975. *(André Bar)*

Naturally, the Mustang IV served with units other than the operational squadrons. The first of them was probably the A&AEE (Aeroplane & Armament Experimental Establishment). Various aircraft were used at different times and among the first was KH648. This aircraft was lost on 19 January 1945. That day, G/C J.F.X. McKenna took off from Old Sarum. It was his first flight in the aircraft. After a couple of minutes the aircraft was seen in a steep dive, with the starboard wing breaking off, leaving no chance of survival for the pilot who crashed near the airfield. It was later discovered that the ammunition panel unlocked during the flight causing a loss of control by destroying the lateral stability and, finally, the right wing. Of course, not all of the flights ended that way and all other Mustang IVs ended their A&AEE career without any major incidents. KH648 had arrived the previous autumn as a sort of back-up for TK589, which had been in use since October, because, as stated in the introduction, TK589 was an early production P-51D and, therefore, a bit different from the ones ultimately delivered to the RAF. TK589 was used until July 1945

31

when it suffered a minor accident and left the A&AEE. It was repaired in August but, with the war over, it was sent to No. 38 MU for storage where it was struck off charge in October 1946. It was replaced by TK588 which had been stored since the previous summer and was issued at the same time as KH766. KH656 arrived in September and both KH766 and TK588 were used until December when flights were terminated. KH656 would have a very short career with the A&AEE and, therefore, with the RAF, as it was damaged in a minor accident just six days after its arrival. Repaired, it was stored and struck off charge in February 1947. As with TK589, TK588 ended its career at No. 38 MU, after arriving in March 1946, and was struck off charge in January 1947. KH766 followed suit the following September. Otherwise, KH704 was used by the AFDS (Air Fighting Development Squadron) between January and May 1945 and ended its career with the CFS (Central Flying Establishment) before going into storage in December. Various other second line units used the Mustang for a while, like the Handling Squadron (KM182 and KM414) and the PRDU (Photographic Reconnaissance Development Unit). Indeed, the RAF, after having used the Mustang Mk.I & II in the tactical reconnaissance role very satisfactorily for three years, and being aware of the tactical reconnaissance version of the P-51D/K (F-6D/K) put to good use by the Americans, had considered the Mustang IV for the same role for the future campaign in the Far East even though the Spitfire FR.14/FR.18 could perform the role perfectly despite its shorter range. KM236 was therefore tested in May and June 1945 by the PRDU. A handful more were used by a couple of second line units and two Mustangs were destroyed. KH777 was lost when a wing hit the ground on overshoot causing the aircraft to swing and hit the dispersal pen at Fairwood Common. The pilot, F/L J. Farmer was injured. KH777 was, at that time, serving with No. 2 APS (Armament Practice Station) and was one of three used by the unit. The other two were KH680 and KM218. During a ferry flight within the UK, one Mustang, KH838, was lost when the ATA pilot decided to undertake aerobatics at low altitude (1,000 feet) contrary to standing orders. The pilot, who was killed, was rather inexperienced on the Mustang, with only two hours logged on type, which may explain the loss of control while attempting too perform a roll. Generally speaking, however, most of the Mustang IVs that stayed in the UK were never issued to any unit. Only 165 or so Mustangs, of the roughly 610 reserved for the UK, had a career with the RAF which explains why the Mustang IV had quite a discreet career.

Date	Pilot	S/N	Origin	Serial	Code	Unit	Fate
19.01.45	G/C John F.X. McKenna	RAF No.05151	RAF	**KH648**		A&AEE	†
15.02.45	3rd Off. Albert E.R. Fairman	-	ATA	**KH838**		3.FP	†
23.04.45	W/C Michel G.L.M. Donnet	RAF No.102522	(BEL)/RAF	**KM121**	MLD	Bentwaters	-
07.09.45	F/L John W.G. Farmer	RAF No.119920	RAF	**KH777**		2.APS	-
14.11.45	W/C Derek R. Walker	RAF No.39952	RAF	**KM232**	JBW	Digby	†

Mustang IV TK589 taken during a test flight with the A&AEE. Its former identity, 44-13332, can still be seen under the stabilisers (see photo p4).

IN MEMORIAM
Mustang IV
(Western Europe)

Name	Service No	Rank	Age	Origin	Date	Serial
Butler, James	RAF No.136573	F/L	*n/k*	RAF	05.04.45	KM137
Casburn, Robert Hardie	RAF No.162938	F/O	24	(US)/RAF	12.05.45	KH644
Davidson, Joseph	RAF No.127915	F/L	32	RAF	04.05.45	KH818
Dick, John Norrie Gordon	Can./J.21907	F/L	23	RCAF	15.04.45	KH764
Fairman, Albert E.R.	-	3rd Off.	23	ATA	15.02.45	KH838
Gihl, Douglas Emil	RAF No.138098	F/L	27	RAF	03.08.45	KH829
Gilberton-Pritchard, John Clare	RAF No.1084862	W/O	*n/k*	RAF	29.03.45	KH651
Lorenz, Sylverster Henry	Can./J.95148	P/O	22	RCAF	10.05.45	KH665
McClung, Vernon Frederick	Can./J.37017	P/O	23	RCAF	18.06.45	KH666
McKenna, John Francis Xavier	RAF No.05151	G/C	39	RAF	19.01.45	KH648
Magdziak, Stanisław	PAF P.782139	F/Sgt	24	PAF	20.08.45	KM201
Natta, Basil Matthew Cameron	NZ422308	P/O	22	RNZAF	04.05.45	KH674
Robson, Robert William	RAF No.49208	F/L	26	RAF	20.06.45	KH664
Rutecki, Alojzy	PAF P.780703	W/O	26	PAF	20.08.45	KM113
Schandler, Jan	PAF P-2428	F/O	25	PAF	02.01.46	KH836
Standrin, Arthur	RAF No.1067443	W/O	23	RAF	29.03.45	KH697
Stewart, Ian Graham	RAF No.43983	S/L	25	RAF	25.03.45	KH732
Stolely, Albert Clifford	RAF No.1805145	F/Sgt	22	RAF	18.12.45	KH707
Sztuka, Konrad	PAF P.704334	W/O	25	PAF	02.01.46	KH747
Walker, Derek Ronald	RAF No.39952	W/C	30	RAF	14.11.45	KM232

Total: 20

Canada: 3, New Zealand: 1, Poland: 4, United Kingdom: 11, USA: 1

n/k: not known

North American Mustang Mk. IVA KM121
Bentwaters Wing
Wing Commander Michel G.L.M. 'Mike' DONNET (Belgium)
Bentwaters (UK), April 1945

North American Mustang Mk. IV KH655
No. 19 Squadron
Flying Officer Edward R. DAVIES
Peterhead (UK), April 1945

North American Mustang Mk. IVA KM148
No. 65 (East India) Squadron
Squadron Leader John W. FOSTER
Bentwaters (UK), June 1945

North American Mustang Mk. IV KH663
No. 303 (Polish) Squadron
Wick (UK), Summer 1945

North American Mustang Mk. IVA KH729
No. 442 (RCAF) Squadron
Squadron Leader Mitchell 'Johnny' JOHNSTON (RCAF)
Digby (UK), June 1945

www.RAF-IN-COMBAT.com

- USN Aircraft 1922-1962 -
- Squadrons! -
- RAF, Dominion and Allied squadrons at War -
- Allied Wings -
- Famous squadrons of WW2 -
- Fighter Leaders -

Printed in Great Britain
by Amazon